Children's Authors

Roald Dahl

Jill C. Wheeler
ABDO Publishing Company

visit us at
www.abdopublishing.com

Published by ABDO Publishing Company, 4940 Viking Drive, Edina, Minnesota 55435.
Copyright © 2007 by Abdo Consulting Group, Inc. International copyrights reserved in all
countries. No part of this book may be reproduced in any form without written permission from
the publisher. The Checkerboard Library™ is a trademark and logo of ABDO Publishing
Company.

Printed in the United States.

Cover Photo: Getty Images
Interior Photos: Corbis pp. 12, 14, 21; © Disney Enterprises, Inc./Roald Dahl Museum and Story
    Center p. 15; Getty Images pp. 17, 19, 23; Photography by Jan Baldwin p. 5; © Quentin
    Blake/Random House UK Limited p. 8; © Roald Dahl Nominee Limited/Roald Dahl
    Museum and Story Center pp. 7, 9, 11, 13

Series Coordinator: Megan Murphy
Editors: Rochelle Baltzer, Megan Murphy
Art Direction: Neil Klinepier

Library of Congress Cataloging-in-Publication Data

Wheeler, Jill C., 1964-
    Roald Dahl / Jill C. Wheeler.
      p. cm. -- (Children's authors)
    Includes bibliographical references and index.
    ISBN-10 1-59679-763-0
    ISBN-13 978-1-59679-763-5
    1. Dahl, Roald--Juvenile literature. 2. Authors, English--20th century--Biography--Juvenile
literature. 3. Children's stories--Authorship--Juvenile literature. I. Title. II. Series.

PR6054.A35Z945 2006
823'.914--dc22

                                                                                2005019536

Contents

In Tune with Kids

Roald Dahl is one of England's most famous children's authors. Many of Dahl's 19 children's books have become international best sellers. The British editions of his books have sold 40 million copies alone. Dahl received hundreds of letters a day from young fans around the world.

Dahl got ideas for books and stories from incidents in his life. He frequently wrote his ideas in an old, worn school notebook. He said almost every story began as a three- or four-line note in that book. Once, he even wrote a one-word story idea in the dust on his car.

Dahl wrote just four hours a day. He worked from 10 AM to noon. Then, he worked again from 4 to 6 PM. He wrote in a tiny brick hut outside his home in rural England.

Most of the time, Dahl scratched out his stories in pencil. He sat in an old armchair with a writing board on his lap. He would work on a book for eight or nine months. A short story might take six months to complete. The rest of the time he raised livestock and bred greyhounds. He also enjoyed growing orchids and working in his garden.

Some people said Dahl's stories were too dark and troubling for children. Dahl disagreed. He said children never complained about his writing. Instead, they giggled and squirmed with delight as they read his fantastical tales.

Dahl was enthusiastic about children becoming readers. He got them hooked by offering them stories they truly wanted to read.

Roald's Family

Roald Dahl was born on September 13, 1916, in Llandaff, Wales. Wales is a small country on the same island as England. Roald's father was a successful businessman named Harald. Harald helped people buy and sell ships.

Roald's mother was named Sofie. She was much younger than Harald. Both of them were born in Norway. In fact, the Dahl family visited Norway each year. Roald grew to think of Norway as his home, too.

Harald had been married before he met Sofie, but his first wife had died. Their two children, Ellen and Louis, were Roald's half sister and half brother. Roald also had two older sisters, Astri and Alfhild, and a younger sister, Else.

Roald was four years old when tragedy struck his family. Astri died of **appendicitis** when she was only seven. Harald died two months later from **pneumonia**. Roald's sister Asta was born soon after. Sofie found herself caring for six young children all on her own.

Roald would grow up to have many of the same interests as both his parents. Like his father, Roald enjoyed paintings, gardening, and woodcarving. And like his mother, Roald said he had "a deep interest in almost everything under the sun."

Witch Tales

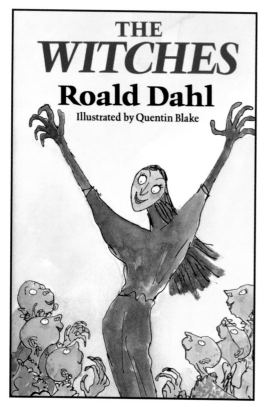

Roald wrote **The Witches** based on stories he heard as a child. Quentin Blake drew the cover illustration for this edition of the book. In fact, Blake illustrated most of Roald's books.

Young Roald enjoyed playing outside. He liked to watch birds and butterflies. Once, he ate a buttercup bulb just to see what it was like. He recalled it tasted very hot. He also used to ride his tricycle so fast that he whizzed around corners on two wheels!

Roald loved books and stories, too. His mother often told tales of trolls and witches. He heard many of these stories on the family's summer trips to Norway. Roald listened carefully. He rarely forgot a story once he heard it.

Some of Roald's childhood experiences showed up in his writing years later. These included an incident at a local sweet shop. Roald and his friends didn't like the two old women who ran the store. They thought the women were witches. Once, the boys hid a dead mouse in one of the candy jars. They were severely punished afterward.

Roald's mother sent him to boarding school at age nine. Harald had thought English schools were the best in the world. Sofie wanted to honor his wishes. So, she sent all of the children away to school. Roald went to St. Peter's Preparatory School in Weston-super-Mare, England.

Roald was always a child at heart. When he had children of his own, he restored this gypsy caravan for them. The caravan was used as the basis for Danny's caravan in **Danny the Champion of the World.**

Scary Schools

The staff members at St. Peter's were very strict. Roald recalled there were "rules, rules and still more rules." Students who broke the rules were beaten with a cane. Roald later wrote about his days at boarding school in an **autobiography** called *Boy*. However, he admitted he **exaggerated** certain situations a bit.

Roald spent four years at St. Peter's. Next, he attended a well-known private school called Repton. The school was in Derbyshire, England.

By that time, Roald's mother had moved to London. The new family home was large. It had tennis courts and a ping-pong table. Roald much preferred being at home. Repton was even more strict than St. Peter's. The headmaster and some of the older boys beat students who broke the rules.

One bright spot at Repton involved a study on chocolate bars. Cadbury used Repton students to help taste test chocolate bars. Roald quickly got hooked. From then on, chocolate bars were one of his favorite treats.

Few at Repton would have guessed Roald had writing talent. His final report card said he did not have a good **vocabulary**. It also said he could not put sentences together very well. Roald said it was no wonder he never thought about becoming a writer until later in life.

Roald excelled at sports at Repton. He was the captain of the squash and handball teams, and he also played football. He enjoyed boxing as well.

Into Africa

Dahl had to decide what he wanted to do after Repton. His mother thought he should go to a university. But, Dahl did not want to do that. He wanted to leave England and travel. So, he spent a summer on a school trip to Newfoundland, Canada. There, he learned how to live in the wilderness.

Dahl returned to England after the summer. In 1934, he took a job with Shell Oil Company. He hoped Shell would send him to Africa or Asia. But at first, he just worked in London. Dahl spent his first four years with Shell living at home. In the evenings, he went out with friends.

But in 1938, Dahl's travel wishes came true. Shell sent him to Dar es Salaam in east Africa. Dahl

Dahl enjoyed his time in Africa working for Shell Oil Company.
Dar es Salaam is in the present-day country of Tanzania.

supplied fuel and **lubricants** to diamond mines and plantations there. He saw many wild animals along the way. Yet, most of the time he sat behind a desk or played sports.

Dahl often listened to the news on the radio. **World War II** loomed. By the time the war began in 1939, Dahl had started to get bored with his job. At 22 years of age, he decided to join the war effort. He traveled to Kenya late that year and **enlisted** in England's Royal Air Force (RAF).

Dahl enjoyed flying in the RAF. But at six feet six inches, he was almost too tall to fit comfortably in a fighter plane.

"A Piece of Cake"

Dahl enjoyed his time training for the RAF. However, his plane crashed in the desert before he even joined the fighting. Dahl narrowly escaped his burning plane. He suffered many injuries. It took months and many surgeries before Dahl recovered.

C.S. Forester

Dahl flew again after his crash. He fought in Greece and Syria. He became a skilled fighter pilot. Dahl shot down many enemy warplanes. Yet his old injuries still bothered him. So, he eventually stopped flying. The RAF sent Dahl to work in Washington, D.C. There, he met a writer named C.S. Forester.

Forester interviewed Dahl about his experiences as a pilot. But, Dahl ended up writing the story instead. He called the story "A Piece of Cake." Forester sent the story to the *Saturday Evening Post*. The magazine bought it and paid Dahl $1,000.

Soon Dahl was writing for other magazines as well. He wrote mostly about his wartime experiences. He later said becoming a writer was a **fluke**. He said he never would have thought of it if someone had not asked him to write.

Dahl wrote his first children's story in 1943. He called it *The Gremlins*. It was about tiny creatures who lived on fighter aircraft and made them crash. Then-First Lady Eleanor Roosevelt read the book to her children. She liked it so much she invited Dahl to the White House. That was how Dahl became friends with President Franklin D. Roosevelt.

Walt Disney (left) wanted to make a movie based on The Gremlins. He even had toys made of Dahl's (right) characters. The movie was never made, but the story was released as a Disney picture book in 1943.

Bedtime Stories to Books

Dahl returned to England in 1945. He spent the next few years writing short stories for grown-ups. He became known for his strange tales with surprise endings.

In 1952, Dahl moved to New York City and lived at a friend's home. Shortly after moving, he attended a dinner party. There, he met a young actress named Patricia Neal.

Roald and Patricia married in 1953. They had five children. Their names were Olivia, Tessa, Theo, Ophelia, and Lucy. Dahl made up bedtime stories for the children. Slowly, those stories would find their way onto paper.

The family was badly shaken in December 1960. A taxi hit baby Theo in his stroller. The boy suffered multiple head injuries. Dahl asked an inventor friend to help make a device for Theo. Eventually, Theo recovered and did not need the device anymore. Yet, the **Dahl-Wade-Till valve** helped many other people with similar problems afterward.

Dahl's career as a children's author took off in 1961. That year, *James and the Giant Peach* was published in the United States. The book is about a boy who travels thousands of miles in a peach the size of a house. The boy makes many strange friends along the way.

Unfortunately, tragedy struck the Dahl family again in 1962. Seven-year-old Olivia died of **complications** from the measles. Dahl had a hard time writing for a while after her death.

Dahl said he never would have been able to write for children if he had not had a family of his own.

Ups and Downs

To the relief of his fans, Dahl did begin writing again. *Charlie and the Chocolate Factory* was published in 1964. The now-famous tale is about a boy who wins a chance to tour a candy factory. Yet, he finds that the factory is not quite as sweet as it may seem.

Charlie and the Chocolate Factory was even more popular than *James and the Giant Peach*. However, not everyone was a fan of Dahl's work. Some **critics** said his children's stories were too violent. People also complained that Dahl portrayed adults as mostly bad people.

Dahl defended his work. He said children like scary tales and frightening situations. He also said they like to see bad things happen to bad people. Dahl believed that was why his books were popular. He also realized that kids get bored easily. He worked to make sure his books were never boring.

The following years brought both success and more tragedy. Dahl's wife, Patricia, suffered three strokes during her pregnancy with their fifth child. Dahl was determined to help her recover. He pushed her very hard to get back to normal. Eventually, she did get better.

Dahl stands outside his writing hut. Inside, Dahl kept a ball of silver paper from all the chocolate bars he ate. He also kept part of the bone the surgeons removed from his leg after his plane crash. He used the bone as a paperweight.

Writing to the End

In addition to books and stories, Dahl also wrote several **screenplays** over the years. Two of his screenplays were based on books by British author Ian Fleming. They were *Chitty Chitty Bang Bang* and the James Bond movie *You Only Live Twice*. Those efforts made Dahl among the best-paid writers in Hollywood.

Dahl's work again made it to Hollywood in 1971. Gene Wilder stars in the first movie version of *Charlie and the Chocolate Factory*. In 1973, Dahl published a **sequel** to the book called *Charlie and the Great Glass Elevator*.

Roald and Patricia divorced in 1983. That same year, he married Felicity Crosland, and the two made their home in England. Soon after, Dahl published three of his most successful books. *The BFG*, *Matilda*, and *The Witches* made him more popular than ever.

In 1990, doctors **diagnosed** Dahl with a rare blood disease. He spent the last months of his life in almost constant pain. He died on November 23, 1990, at the age of 74.

After his death, Dahl's books remained popular. In 1996, *James and the Giant Peach* was made into a movie. *The Witches* was produced onstage in England in summer 2005. Also that summer, Warner Brothers released a new movie based on *Charlie and the Chocolate Factory*. Today, Roald Dahl's fanciful work continues to gain new fans.

In addition to being honored with two movie versions of **Charlie and the Chocolate Factory,** *Dahl received several literary awards. He won the British Literary Award in 1983. And in 1988, he won the Children's Book Award for* **Matilda.**

Glossary

appendicitis - a response to injury or irritation of the appendix that is usually accompanied by swelling and severe pain, with possible risk of a burst appendix. The appendix is the part of the intestines in the lower right-hand portion of the body.

autobiography - a story of a person's life that is written by himself or herself.

complication - a second condition that develops as a result of a primary disease or condition.

critic - a professional who gives his or her opinion on art, literature, or performances.

Dahl-Wade-Till valve - a tube inserted into the skull to reduce the amount of pressure and fluid on the brain.

diagnose - to recognize something by signs, symptoms, or tests, such as a disease.

enlist - to join the armed forces.

exaggerate - to make something seem larger or greater than it is.

fluke - accidental luck.

lubricant - a substance used to reduce friction between moving parts, such as grease or oil.

pneumonia - a disease that affects the lungs and may cause fever, coughing, and chest pain.

screenplay - the script for a movie.

sequel - a book or movie continuing a story that began previously.

vocabulary - a list or collection of words and phrases used by an individual.

World War II - from 1939 to 1945, fought in Europe, Asia, and Africa. Great Britain, France, the United States, the Soviet Union, and their allies were on one side. Germany, Italy, Japan, and their allies were on the other side.

Web Sites

To learn more about Roald Dahl, visit ABDO Publishing Company on the World Wide Web at **www.abdopublishing.com**. Web sites about Dahl are featured on our Book Links page. These links are routinely monitored and updated to provide the most current information available.

Index